THE 9-DAY QUEEN GETS LOST

ON HER WAY TO THE EXECUTION

THE 9-DAY QUEEN GETS LOST
ON HER WAY TO THE EXECUTION

poems by
Karyna McGlynn

Acme Poem Company
Willow Springs Books
Spokane, Washington

ACKNOWLEDEMENTS

The author would like to thank the editors of the following journals where some of the poems in this book first appeared, sometimes in earlier forms or with different titles.

Caketrain: "Why it slides down the adder."
Coconut: "The 9-day queen gets lost on her way to the execution," "Don't look me full in the mahogany dimension of this."
Denver Quarterly: "My melancholic circuitry doesn't mean."
Devil's Lake: "Prereq."
FENCE: "This old man, he will take me out in a taxi."
Interrupture: "Though she said it was only a fishing village."
LIT: "Her head was blacker than coal, she didn't mind."
NOÖ Journal: "There are worse things than chastity, Mr. Shannon."
Octopus: "I trisected the bull's bladder in lavender."
Quarterly West: "To find tentacle porn reprehensible."
RealPoetik: "The room folded in gelid light."
Spork: "Since you already have a diminutive nude in your glass."

The 9-Day Queen Gets Lost on Her Way to the Execution is Volume 6 in the Acme Poem Company Surrealist Poetry Series.

Cover Art: *Op. 2 No. 4* and *Op. 2 No. 5* by Josh Urban Davis. 17"x12," watercolor and ink on paper. This and other works by Josh Urban Davis can be found at http://juddavis88.wix.com/joshurbandavis.

Cover Design: Clarinda Simpson
Interior Design: Alia Bales and Jess Bryant

FIRST EDITION

Willow Springs Editions, Spokane, WA 99202
Copyright © 2016 by Karyna McGlynn
Printed in the United States of America
All Rights Reserved
Printed by Gray Dog Press
ISBN: 978-0-9832317-9-0

This and other Willow Springs Books may be viewed online at www.willowspringsbooks.org.

—for my queens, Josh & Analicia

CONTENTS

Angèle: I'll be punished?

Mr. Oscar: Yes, your punishment, my poor Angèle, is to be you.
To have to live with yourself.

     -Holy Motors (2012)

I'M NOT SAYING IT'S IMPOSSIBLE

but I did go through the smaller door inside the garden shed—
shit, it just doesn't admit much...

watch this, I want you to see when I slip
my hand under the black lace of language & nude-like stuff underneath

do you understand "too little space on the manor of me"?
though hot, though mindless & *lordy, lordy, lordy*

will you do
when I prop my boots & shoot my mouth, you unschooled in quailing
women of elaborate hairdo or fat vocabulary

no, my lead surveys the burnt out
shell of Strindberg & stretches his back in the wings

...somebody raise him into my world on tethers & tongs

comme ça my interest wheels out its sweating horse
comme ça my heart lower its boom

& stoops to concur

MY MELANCHOLIC CIRCUITRY DOESN'T MEAN

Because, lovely, there is an abundance

of something in me, if only black bile

you accumulate, too: some sloe-eyed

botanical…what did you get away with?

Your cutaway eddies with fume of almond.

Your mouth is a cupping glass, resinous, this

funicular gift—my spine, your prick, are we

already married? In this copper oil, in this

fumarole room: your irredeemable slovenly

heart melancholic—my bones make esses

and esses and esses, your head turns heavy

blue and veined with milk: I ask you what's

in the jar? My toebox snuffs the fine print:

I've often thought your hands were made to

kill canaries in a yellow furl of your tendency.

My melancholic circuitry doesn't mean—

………all the almonds, almonds, almonds!

HOT SHALLOWS THE COLOR INFIRMARY WALLS

are swaddled nurses get lost on a straight line

                     of course, white babies

are men oily dings sur la plage

                     vultures steal puppies

which ward is too hot to let her hair down

                     call this prop "parasol"

which color of near-blindness

                     in the jungle lining

are girl too sick or half in love with why

                     her swimcap discarded

which tooth in a jar of baby

                     apple rattles & mutters

which word like "pistachio ice cream"

                     on the blonde comb

argues gently inside the dead langue

                     with a strand of saliva

THE ROOM FOLDED IN GELID LIGHT

there was a wrought iron hole in my body
from my bed the retractor looked far away

I fingered the grillwork, the cool hard
lips of the thing someone said had teeth

might bite my finger, somebody said
don't touch now, germs, in any case

mea culpa, what was I doing trapped
in a storm drain in the first place

somebody said I must be patient now
patient as patio furniture

it was out of my hands
there were eggs stuck in my iron mouth

my head swayed, an airy addendum
the soft shells pulsed like shrapnel

they were lodged in my coal hole
somebody said, Say you are only a house

I am only a house—Good, now
breathe out—*no, out*—*no, out*

I TRISECTED THE BULL'S BLADDER IN LAVENDER

it was full of etchings & old invitations
some rusted paisley inlet I couldn't
put my finger on the alchemy of what
I was doing despite the spiritualists of
1912 who threw me an EZE castrator
I saw their oily fingers soldered inside
kidskin and didn't believe them a lick
but a man of god said strips of rubber
around my breasts would do the trick
if tied off correctly then lifted my dress
left cupping glasses on my buttocks
where he touched me his talk was thin
as piano wire he showed me his vials
of salve & doused me with toilet water
turned vinegar in what once was a bed
of lavender I marked myself with bull
urine though the man of god insisted
I'd gone straight down now that I was
sunk as an orange blossom billet when
the bull lowed with sweat in my grip

TO FIND TENTACLE PORN REPREHENSIBLE

he said, is to admit an ignorance—or *worse*—
hypocritical love of Chihulian chandeliers, which

                              in their awful prehensility

being uncanny replicas of the proboscidean and—let's face it—
Japanese monsters of light & nipple & bulbous bloodshot

                              if you use your peripheral vision
eeling just over your shoulder,
which are not so much monsters, but rather
                              repositories of information

nightmares which follow us a little behind and to the left—
all undulating eyes and exposed vein—
                              we'd rather not look at head-on

In the West we're more familiar with parables like
The Picture of Dorian Gray—in effect
                              cloaking, stifling, privatizing

what we've turned from our own gourded lusts—
instead of locking up, let levitate out of step
                              floating over/under the ferns

something orange & unexploded: seed, sori, suckers—
Fig. I—see this amber one here?
                              it's yours—doesn't take an expert to

Note the multiplicity of hammerheads, the ivory
swordfish filleted along the tatami floor mats
                              go low on slender creeper ankles
that are—need we say it?—ribbed
but differentiated in that someone
                              —God knows who, or why—

has attempted to interject—yes, to *comb*—
through the fellated beer tresses of the undertow

which filled the whole room

but then just kept growing over/under the calcium
deposits of its own best intentions and

"rein it in," remain modest

despite the throne it's built for itself, this smoky
pulsing thing the uneducated might be tempted

to call "a tumor in the ballroom"

PREREQ

Can't tell why but I'm required to
love each of the men in this room…

> —she caught her breath like she was going
> to slip "you sl…" but pulled the wings off

instead turned inward / a blanched peach (the way women do)
in her batik print dress

> the long-legged ermine of patience (no, tact)

got up from the table, excused itself

I put this bonbon in my mouth / think it's full of crude

What I wanted to say is wearing sexier pants / moving away from me
like a black Madonna, not my heritage

> I checked under the plucked typewriter key / each man's scrotum

> —she had a look like "hel-*lo*, I'm here…?"

I'm sorry, I said
(rapping my knuckle against each testicle)
I'm trying to find where my will resides

THERE ARE WORSE THINGS THAN CHASTITY, MR. SHANNON

I remember those twilight zone gals propped around him:
old mannequins gesticulating something very nearly *like* love,
he can't complain: an overpowering aroma:
plutonian roe in my cheek where an old glow spikes
the drunk struck bell of me, backing off,
damping desire back its damn buttonhole, mincing the full of me
up with mallet and cleaver
                    to make a more malleable plaything.
Agh, the most miserable lizard bourbons his doorstep,
loses my mind in his woodpile.
                    Thus, I've buckled the brunt of my want
in this old train-case—tagged it in the prop room
for some winsome moment of intrepidity: *All women,*
whether they wish to admit it or not,
       would like to get men into a tied-up situation…
What is this
unknown thing which feathers the line of my lipstick,
warrens into my estranged genes like *gimme gimme gimme*

THOUGH SHE SAID IT WAS ONLY A FISHING VILLAGE

her mouth befuddled me   why she felt the need

    to tell me her genes   spangled in taxidermy

       know me so well   or how I feel about

          cussing & crawfish   to say as if in shame

             every woman's   trousseau comes

       with an ancient dish   of Brach's butterscotch

     candy she is forever   obliged to offer me

   saying there's a small   artillery under the sofa

ruffle & to preface with   I hope you like wild turkey

    or even have to ask   whether you brought

       apricot nail polish   remover & a push-up

         bra if you can bear to   stomach the thought

           like I'd ever refuse   a Newport from

       a relative stranger   or mind old men

        rubbing DEET   behind my knees

    over losing a game   of badminton we'll go

& clean his old boat   & sleep on this foldout

   with pepperoni hiccups   & QVC flickering

      in earnest only without   sound the overworked

        icemaker trembling   in the sunburst kitchen

          sleepless like I might   not love the dog

IT HAD NO LIGHTS OR LUMINOUS TISSUES

the thing wasn't Robert Taylor
slapping me awake in sepia

I didn't come to, consumptive

mouth all wrong, drooping at
the corners, but startled by my

animus: my monstrous ingénue

wardrobe—it flipped a penny
heads it said: now you had better

get in the jeep or I'll hurt you

understand? your body is now
property of my pain fantasy

believe me, blond bitch

bend over the mahogany chair,
expose your buttocks to the brand:

white oak leaf seared into my hip

I cried out, I turned to look at it:
emaciated, brainwashed, pathetic

a 90 lb. accountant spitting sand

in the face of a fellow sufferer—
I'm not the one you want, I said

its mouth grew whip-thin & pious

said, you can be ____ed or ____ed
for what you've done to me, but

what was it that I did? I asked

a rash decision spread rapidly
over the room, answered back

too quickly, this ersatz officer

eyeing me, this high plains drifter
astride the bloodshot boomtown

of my gut, my bad impulses

which stared me straight down
a milelong sight, a cocked gun

WHAT THIS THING IN THE DARK WHEAT ROCKING

no, I cannot undermine

           this cross-stitch
           this ice-dart

(she pulled her knees to her chest
and faced the storm: a gargoyle mounted
           the back of the house)

there was no tongue
or wings
or bulging cartilage
           just a brimming thing
           a hefting
           pooled in shot
and needled

(the dark air filling, the yeast strain dazzling,
the night sky boiling to a point)

           a prod
nudged blunt
against the thing unyielding in the wet wheat

           (as the first
the fat drops slapped the field
like spoonfuls of flesh)

THE 9-DAY QUEEN GETS LOST ON HER WAY TO THE EXECUTION

If ever a bathtub was Klee's *Bacchanal in Rotwein*, this was it:

16 years after the 6th grade, Jane Grey & her junior high tormentors
played "I'll show you mine if you'll show me yours"

        …but this was their Saturn Returns

She explained this: they were all at their most beautiful
that moment a thrown object hovers weightless at its apex

        but, *furthermore*

"diametrically opposed sex is only safe for animals & the highly evolved—"

Whenever she spoke, one bowed, the other said "okay, Ms. Dictionary—"
Like she was a porpoise laid clean, sliced, still glistening on the bed sheet

        they serviced her, in multiple dimensions—

their child parts felt their blind way out the school doors & up
nudging their blunt, indelicate ways into the future
in which what they *wanted* was suddenly permissible:

        why apologize in the face of these lovely reversals?

"I am an impenetrable fortress"

She said it then, now she says it again, but it was *& never will be* the case

SAFETY IS ALARMINGLY

easy to disarm, or drain from the room

Her *certain*
went out quiet as vodka / nothing could sustain it

                                        where it went
down past the baseboards
                                        where it went
past the air-kiss of her infant
horse descending its brass pole / ending it there

She arrived from her dress on a stage in tangerine & pink light:
There's nothing you can do to stop me

One stroke took the air out of thing inanimate: we saw
structures / fixtures crumple like newly grieved faces:

There's nothing you can do to stop me

Perhaps this was her due historical tincture / blood loosed
like a scarf down a glass of—what—water?

What did she expect to *do* undiluted, antediluvian?

                                        where it went
lacing the base of odorless tumblers

Outside, the pressure continued to drop its dry clothes
but inside, swallowing, something less obvious, hissing

SINCE YOU ALREADY HAVE A DIMINUTIVE NUDE IN YOUR GLASS

she said, *I'm leaving now*

he looked at her through his gin funnel

she was nude & scarred & not at all appealing

he opened some applejack against his boot

his top hat fell off, he dropped his ice tongs

three members of the commedia dell'arte frowned

his goat was clearly pissed & too afraid to show it

though his wife was half out the door

there was a relic garnishing the rim of his aperitif

a blonde kneeling, her onion breasts floating

& besides there was a dead woman in organza

lying under the piano bench, or was it his wife

passed out again for shame or carnations

HER HEAD WAS BLACKER THAN COAL, SHE DIDN'T MIND

the stuffy inefficiency or the fact his eyes
were slot like a goat's so long as he didn't
mind the fact she didn't have arms & he
didn't mind her chain-smoking or care that
she was only a bust so long she didn't mind
his brilliantined hair or the way he turned
up his moustache with earwax or why all the
lights were out so long he didn't mind the
coral sinkhole of her lips or the idea she was
so lidless but why would he when he was
wearing a bathing suit & wouldn't offer her
a drink in fear it would stain the plum
viscera of the oriental rug when he didn't
know yet whether such a woman could even
breed so he was getting himself ready just in
case she was spitting patent muskmelon
seeds into the ashtray or was it tar off her
tongue & did he mind if it was black as roe
when she kept staring at the ticking clock on
the icebox that was at least as big as his head

DON'T LOOK ME FULL IN THE MAHOGANY DIMENSION OF THIS

Just a minute, I swear

           —be smart.

my makeshift skirt lifts me up to yield

           —one foot
           dingo, no
           hippo, no
           hooves but
           not a horse's

broken on a knee

      a bisuccubal tongue

           —be still.

the sub-marine step of his bedroom eyes

a putto's toes graze

           —a red tentacle
           not an elephant's
           trunk coiling
           not a squid's
           jelly arm unfurling

 to ply anything hypoxic

           —my crown.
           his crown
           —look this way
           look that way

don't look me full in the mahogany dimension of this

           —stop dissembling.

don't relock…pomegranate shivved violent on my eye

BECAUSE MY LEGS ARE GLITTERED IN TINY FANGS OF DEPRESSION GLASS

there are things I just can't say in the back of an El Camino
talk comes unwieldy swings   from my mind on a slipshod
system of pulleys through   my great grandmother's room
my boyfriend steps over   her still body like a rolled carpet
hoists anything of hers   under his wet armpit & ties a rope
around it, casts it out   through the studio's broken French
doors, asks me how   much each plate is worth even though
the room is fouled   with old roach traps & Arm & Hammer
& I don't dare say   the sets have been broken up in my flesh
for sixteen years   or how her late husband stole these plates
from the back of a stopped train, or how I come from a long line of looters
birthed in the backseats of El Caminos—the leather slick with calf's foot jelly

THIS OLD MAN, HE WILL TAKE ME OUT IN A TAXI

under the tunnel
which vertebrates hum
                              large fowl sunk to the bottom

an augmented vinyl interior:
this is where she stitches together or my umbrella
drips with cheap spice rum on the backseat

                              & this spare zygote in your boot
is also me speeding to & from continence

                              & she is on the shadow shelf
                              & she is in the tinder box

light sucked here much slower to get where it's going
                              I cleared my throat until this ladled

where to? well Lowell had a last drink snapped down & out of it

                              I'd never say nipped in the bud
                              but stroked stem: how do you say

a cassé? accreted change lolling off the leather á la milk dug do

A BRIEF CONVEYANCE IN THE VICTORIAN CAR

what else to say about how I came to fall asleep
in the backseat full of petrol & elder-daemons?
How he buckled me inside the shell, *a mere formality*,
moist hand passing over worn velveteen nap?
How as I shut down, the car started up, *a coincidence?*
My tongue stuck thick & coated with rosin—

The street & my stupor grew so steep
I couldn't bear to ask the driver about the fire, my fare—
When we arrived, the parking was permanent—
He led me up the back stairs but I couldn't see beyond
all the black tarp & urban legends scrawled above:

> *the lying boys will speak*
> *& rise if you can summon*
> *the power of a Christian name*

over the idling motor of eighteen hundred &

floor it—

from headboard   *to baseboard*

the match-heads of kids once lit & let out of sight
now hoarded by the Maker of the Victorian Car
who admits only

one occupation at a time—

APRÈS, THE SLUICE THEN THE HOOK

the one truth of the sluice is   *nothing*

a sudden gaff from the present: *nearly like*
pleasure, aloft on the high twin bed
of your single, bodily craft, genital colored   *satin quilt*
in the glamyr of unelectric lamplight
there is a single way: smells like   *pondwater*

so you nose-dive absolute through   *the solution*
occluded by a cloche of predetermination
like a retrofit caul or swim cap   *pulled down*
over your mortal agency, don't move
against the sluice, let it move you through   *the blind*
muscle memory of every deed
made flesh, shades gambling   *one big tell*
over a crash of blackened war bonds

WAITING ROOMS OF THE AVIAN WORLD

"my mother was supposed to meet me here"

                                    that's what they all say—

the visitors who float down our halls
facedown on the hyacinth rugs in the lobby

                 feigning sense of smell

who, similarly, fell down through tobacco stain windows

like stricken pigeons boding bad luck as they enter the house
they don't see the resemblance between *thy* and *thou*

they beg the question
whether pigeons are dying in all the dark parts
chopped down from the perineum of our industry

                this is the talk they busy themselves with

rubbing sleep from their eyes with century-old newsprint

like nickels, they fall
with the same putty impression from the sill, indiscriminate

but will not issue forth a single statement
to illuminate the space where their mother simply *isn't*

UNBURDENING THREE PELTS INTO THE GREASE FIRE

I pursue the hem of what it means to consume
eternally, time don't mean much—

being the once bad spider I have to consider
my former inclinations with meat & silk
bone unmanned, discrete collections: small, uncountable

fur snaps, licked off the flesh!

how I affixed my position fast, shell buttons down my shroud
but it bothers me, somehow, my sprung
lust irreversible, bell lording its Rube Goldbergian sway

of what I am chained to by virtue of scale, *perspective*
my own unmaking snapped into plastic place
around me, chutes, pulleys, baited meat hooks

So what if I
appeared unaccountable at the mouth of the butcher
blinking flour, put out, burning a single degree?

VARIORUM

a fox's pelt velvet crosses a museum's cold span
midnight on its hind legs looks like a punctured   *—what glows in the dark?*

... orange blossom centrifugal in a bottle of ink
a vanilla orchid lopped erotic along a carrot rind   *—what has a makeshift*
                                            bonnet & somewhere to go?

or the fox bellying in from a storm, his stomach
full of sheepdog, whey dripping on my only coal   *—what has 2-dimensions &*
                                            abundant gravitas?

the fox has somewhere to... pulls a makeshift hat
darkly down, Christ, I saw a jacket flicker open   *—what am I tearing my knees*
                                            to get at now?

inside him it looked like this: three amber clocks
up which my smallest buggeries scuttled, rapt inri   *—why is the unchecked center*
                                            of grief gastronomical?

when I peel back the skin I remember the state of my
vegetable soul & meaning gazes up like potato soup   *—my God, who is after*
                                            the throats of the chickens

still steaming in the mouth of my future indiscretions
                                            —who is so very interchangeable

WHY IT SLIDES DOWN THE ADDER

when every green D slides
down into its eventuality: *thankful, loveless*

a water-headed mink
behind the driftwood   slides under my knee
                                    and waits like a vein

to skin me cold, to undo the Ds down my passage

words tethered to an antiquity which also slips!
from a footing less exact
the bounty which gathers above me, avian hunters

This is for his head   this water on it
                                    this knot bag body
a woolen stocking
                        slung on a low snowed fence
I meant, I mean, I…

can't recap the bottle-green of my long undone Ds
the slipping fabric / cut on the bias / the tenuous grip

                        that adder had
                        upon me

all along, mink's broad blue head upending

        own mouth   ,own knee   ,oh

ACME POEM COMPANY

Willow Springs Books is a small literary press under the direction of Christopher Howell and Polly Buckingham. It is housed in Eastern Washington University's Inland Northwest Center for Writers in Spokane. Its annual chapbook series selects and publishes contemporary surrealist poetry under the auspices of the Acme Poem Company.

PREVIOUS COLLECTIONS

Startle Pattern, Larissa Szporluk
Drunk on Salt, James Nolan
You Won't Need That, Robert Gregory
Gnawing on a Thin Man, Ray Amorosi
No Time for Dancing, Adam Hammer

For a complete list of selections from Willow Springs Books and ordering information visit www.willowspringsbooks.org

Willow Springs staff contributors to this chapbook were Alia Bales, Jess Bryant, Andrew Koch, Clarinda Simpson, and Nick Thomas.